READ! A How-to-Guide for Tutors and Parents

Sarah K. Gardner

READ! A How-to-Guide for Tutors and Parents

Copyright © 2017 by Sarah K. Gardner

Published by

Kingdom Kaught Publishing, LLC
Denton, Maryland U.S.A.

Printed in the U.S.A.

All rights reserved. No part of this book may be reproduced or transmitted in any form or by any means, electronic or mechanical, including photocopying, recording or by any information storage and retrieval system without written permission from the author and publisher, except for the inclusion of brief quotations in a review. This author takes responsibility for manuscript errors.

Copy- Editing: Sarah Gardner

Editor: Ebonni Beharry

Graphic Designer: Colin Beharry

ISBN: 978-0-9982100-1-8

Library of Congress Control Number: 2016960128

Table of Contents

Introduction 1

The 20 Keys to Teaching Reading 5

Key #1 - Does He Want to Learn to Read? 7

Key #2 - Check Hearing and Eyesight 9

Key #3 - Plan Short, Positive and Fun Activities 11

Key #4 - Engage All the Senses and Learning Styles 13

Key #5 - Learn the Alphabet in Order and Randomly 15

Key #6 - Students Must Associate Sounds with Letters 19

Key #7 - Learn Consonant Blends and Vowels 23

Key #8 - Learn to Hear Short Vowel Sounds First 25

Key #9 - Use PVC Phone Tool When Teaching Sounds 27

Key #10 - Learn to Hear Long Vowel Sounds Last 29

Key #11 - Learn Sight and Glue Words 31

Key #12 - Learn to Associate Mental Pictures with Words 35

Key #13 - Keep Learning Fun with Positive Reinforcement 37

Key #14 - Guide Thinking Before, During and After Reading 39

Key #15 - Incorporate Capitalization and Punctuation 41

Key #16 - Build on Prior Knowledge and Life Experiences 43

Key #17 - Using Repetition and Summarization 47

Key #18 - Writing Starter: Incomplete Stories and Pictures 49

Key #19 - Oral Reading is Necessary to Build Fluency 53

Key #20 - Teach Comprehension, Spelling and Writing 55

Learning Difficulties: Dyslexia, Dyscalculia, and Dysgraphia 57

Reading Tools and Games 63

Moving Forward 73

How to Get Rid of Test-taking Anxiety 75

Note from the Author 79

A Typical Tutor's Question 83

An Adult Student's Perspective 87

Annotated Book References 89

Photo Credits 93

Website Credits 97

Acknowledgements 99

Author's Bio 101

Dedication

To those who truly want to read and those who want to help, *"For with God nothing shall be impossible"* (Luke 1:37, King James Version).

Introduction

Have you thought about how someone learns to read? What is the process, and how does one determine exactly when reading occurs? The answers to these questions will vary as much as the type of audience and individuals asked. Although to some, learning to read seems to happen like magic, yet others may struggle during the process. I've written READ! *A How-To-Guide for Tutors and Parents* to give practical techniques to anyone who wants to help another learn to read. Any reader who has patience and compassion can become a tutor, especially after you have read this book.

Children routinely spend three or more years learning the makeup of the English language through immersion of sounds, letters, pictures and songs. Generally, this time period begins with parents and continues with pre-school and kindergarten teachers before the child enters the formal school setting. Playing to learn has a positive effect on a child's reading skills because children learn through games.

Children and adults who have trouble reading might not have received this unstructured timeframe of learning to read as they played when they were young. They may also struggle with some form of learning disability or dyslexia (including dyscalculia and dysgraphia, which I will discuss, later). It is my belief that READ! *A How-To-Guide for Tutors and Parents* (directed toward teaching struggling readers the concepts of reading) will empower the reader to help anyone who needs to learn to read, or needs to learn to read better.

From the 1950s until now, the methods of teaching reading vary from sight words and rote learning to phonemic awareness and phonics to the whole-brain learning experience and a mixture of all these methods. You may recall seeing movies of students being taught in one-room schoolhouses, or had a similar experience yourself with printed materials.

I remember sitting at a table with four or five of my classmates as the teacher had each one of us read one sentence from the old "Alice and Jerry" reading books. We were taught to look at and remember each word. This rote learning method was totally different from the phonics method of teaching reading, and the whole brain learning experience. My mother and siblings set great examples as good readers as they frequently discussed the stories they were reading. Books and stories were read to me as a small child, and I visited the library often. I wanted to read, and I liked stories about animals, adventures and travel to distance places. I liked savoring the words of each story as long as there wasn't a time constraint on having to read. Teachers considered me to be an excellent reader because I studied and did my homework each night, so that I would be prepared for class the next day. It seemed like I had a photographic memory.

Unfortunately, my standardized Reading Comprehension scores in the 4th grade were under the 50 percentile range. I could remember what I read silently in a non-testing situation, but during tests it was apparent that I didn't understand what I'd just read. I could call out the words, but I didn't comprehend sentences that were longer than three or four words in a testing situation! I had to relearn reading strategies that incorporated a variety of methods to gain understanding and enjoyment from the written word. I was also terrified of having to read aloud. Instead of concentrating on what I was reading, my mind felt threatened by my listeners.

Although, I sometimes stumbled over a word when reading aloud, I wasn't a struggling reader. I wasn't dyslexic, either, and I didn't have trouble recognizing letters or words or making a connection with sounds. I simply had stage fright that caused me to panic and not be quite fluent when reading in front of other people.

Introduction

I loved books then, and I love books, now. In READ! *A How-To-Guide for Tutors and Parents* I have brought together the variety of methods and strategies that are available to make it easier for students of *any age,* but especially the adult student, to learn to read, today. I believe that it is easier to teach an adult to read because he or she can communicate better his or her issues with the written word, especially in a one-to-one tutoring session.

Tutors can explain and make lessons relevant to the life experiences of the adult (or student of any age) to make reading more understandable.

Adults learn in a variety of ways, and more easily through their dominant senses. Commercial advertisers and businesses like casinos take advantage of this fact. Casinos are masters of the multi-sensory experience, and so is television and cinema. These advertisers use a lot of different colors, animated graphics, sounds, and movement to appeal to our senses and hopefully, get us to REMEMBER and buy their products and services.

Likewise, as tutors, we need to recognize that reading can be taught through a variety of ways, and use the multi-sensory approach to teach our students, regardless of their ages. There are emerging computerized technologies that are easily accessible today. We can show students how to see, hear, touch, taste, and move while reading with these technologies. Computers are available for use in local libraries and in some senior citizen centers as well. Tutors and students can use earbuds or headsets to listen to reading selections, games, and quizzes. It is okay for the tutor to do most of the work in accessing and starting each computer program until the student gets the hang of it.

Adding five minutes of an interesting audio/visual clip that you can watch, stop, and discuss is a great way to motivate a student, and energize or animate a written lesson. The point is to find the resource that works best for your student to keep learning to read, write and spell fun and interesting.

I want everyone to learn to read because reading affects all the other academic subjects, such as: writing, spelling, social studies, science and mathematics. One must know how to read effectively in order to improve in all other subjects of schoolwork. I wish every reader who struggles could have a year of personal tutoring tailored to his or her individual needs BEFORE the third grade, but it is not too late to learn to read as an adult!

Today, we are in the digital age using computers, tablets, e-readers, smartphones, and other devices that make learning to read an audio-visual tactile experience. In order to keep up with progress, all students whether young or old have to be able to read and access information quickly. I wrote this book to provide quick practical steps to help more people become tutors who want to assist someone in learning to read.

I've provided a balanced, fun and systematic approach that includes visuals and games to teach reading, spelling, and writing. I believe in the whole-brain system of teaching that involves all of a student's senses. When students are fully involved in the lesson with hands-on techniques the yawning stops and their interest awakens. The process of learning to read is a matter of finding the right "key" to the student's understanding.

I believe you can teach someone how to read. I also believe it doesn't matter if a student is 5 or 105, if he wants to learn. You (the parent, teacher or tutor) can take steps to improve their reading. I believe you can do it using the following 20 "KEYS" to reading: **K**eep [**R**eading] **E**xciting **Y**et **S**imple.

The 20 Keys to Teaching Reading

I.] Students must want to learn to read, and have fun learning.
II.] Students should get their eyesight and hearing tested.
III.] Tutors should keep activities short and positive.
IV.] Multi-sensory learning styles must be used in lessons.
V.] The Alphabet is learned in order, randomly, and viewed from left to right.
VI.] Students must associate sounds with letters.
VII.] Students must learn consonant blends and vowels.
VIII.] Students must learn to hear short vowel sounds first.
VIX.] Tutors can use PVC Phones when teaching sounds.
X.] Students must learn to hear long vowel sounds last.
XI.] Students must learn sight and glue words.
XII.] Students should learn to associate mental pictures with words.
XIII.] Tutors should use positive reinforcement and praise to make learning fun.
XIV.] Tutors should tell students what to think about before, during, and after reading by asking: Why, When, Where, What, Who and How?
XV.] Incorporate Capitalization and Punctuation in lessons.
XVI.] Stories and writing should build on prior knowledge and life experiences.
XVII.] Tutors should use repetition in reading passages, comprehension questions, and summarization to ascertain students' understanding.

XVIII.] Action pictures and incomplete stories are great writing starters.
XIX.] Oral reading is necessary to build fluency.
XX.] Teach Comprehension, Spelling and Writing, simultaneously.

Key #1 - Does He Want to Learn to Read?

Does your student want to learn to read, or is someone forcing him to come to class? Half of the process of learning to read can be overcome if the student is motivated to try. The students who take a book everywhere they go will usually get practice in reading it.

Add "fun" reading selections to your tutoring sessions… jokes, riddles, silly sayings, amusing pictures, and funny or weird newspaper articles, comic books, etc., to stimulate a students' interest. Both children and adults like playing games, so make a game of learning to read in grocery stores, on the road, or anywhere.

I like using silly voices for each character and putting my finger on each word as I read stories to my grandchildren. They giggle, laugh a lot, and shout, "Read it again!" They also tell me if I forget a word, sentence or sequence in the stories.

From birth to preschool, children are immersed in reading games with their caregivers, usually mothers, but sometimes fathers, siblings, and others are involved. Being read to or playing words games and using songs and silly rhymes engages children mentally in the spoken and written language. Children begin to learn and understand new vocabulary without really trying.

A more condensed method can be used in a like manner to convey balanced reading concepts when teaching adults. The difference is the material used; adult readers need to work with meaningful and relevant material. Readers want to have fun while learning, so *Keep Reading Exciting, Yet Simple!*

Key #2 - Check Hearing and Eyesight

I read an incredible library book, <u>Why Can't U Teach Me 2 Read?</u> by Beth Fertig, in which four students with learning disabilities fought the New York Public School system and won! Three of the four students were from the Dominican Republic, and no one had addressed the hearing and vision problems that they had. Eventually, they found tutors to help them target and mitigate their learning difficulties.

Has your student's hearing and vision been checked lately? Some students with learning disabilities may need glasses or hearing aids or other directions toward understanding the printed word. It is also easier to tell the difference between the letters of the alphabet when one can see clearly. Some letters look alike with the tails, circles, dots and sticks going in different directions, so it's important to be able to recognize similarities and differences. It is equally important to be able to hear the sounds that the individual letters, blends and words make as the English language is spoken or read, orally.

Past research has shown that using tools like colored transparencies, rulers, triangles, graphic organizers, pointers, and PVC pipes to soften glaring lighting, highlight words and sentences, and amplify sound are very helpful in training the eyes and ears to follow lines of written type. In the English language, students have to be taught to read from the left to the right, and top to the bottom of words and pages.

I was asked to tutor a young man who was attending a family-oriented workshop at my church. After questioning him, I found that the problem was his eyesight. He held the paper up to his nose because he needed bifocals to even see the 36-point font size words that I had printed on paper. He had broken his eyeglasses, and was waiting for new ones.

Key #3 - Plan Short, Positive and Fun Activities

Fun strategies can be taught in 5 or 10-minute sessions to keep students from getting frustrated with lessons. Tutors should be alert to their students' attention spans, and have a variety of short interesting lessons planned that are tailored to their students' learning styles. The paragraphs below describe some fun strategy ideas.

Create sentences and cut them into individual words to use as puzzles. Put labels on items in the room. Look for words on signs and buildings as you drive through neighborhoods and business districts. Read the labels on cans, packages, and aisle markers at the grocery store. Create fill-in the blank sentences, and play opposite-word games with your students.

Go to the library to read book titles and covers to try to guess what the book is about. Ask your student to dictate five words that could be used as descriptions (colors, shapes, numbers, other adjectives, etc.), while you write them down. You and your student can use those words to create a story or description of something. It can be silly, serious, sad or funny; you are only limited by your imagination!

I used a sentence from a favorite storybook of one young boy, and I added his name to it. Then I cut the sentence into words, and asked him to put the sentence back together. We also used other words to make the sentence silly. He loved this activity!

It is very important that students practice reading for five or ten minutes, daily. You can encourage a student to do this by reading the first part of a colorful interesting book *to them*, and have the student read the rest to or with you. It's also important to give *lots of praise* to students for their efforts during this time! I love seeing students smile when I tell them that they are excellent readers.

Key #4 - Engage All the Senses and Learning Styles

The many ways students use their senses to learn new information is known as learning styles. It is important that you discover your student's preferred learning style(s) and use associated materials in lessons. As a tutor, you want to learn to teach in a variety of styles to keep lessons fun and entertaining for students. Students may use one or a combination of the following styles to learn:

1. **Visual:** Does your student prefer to see colorful material?
2. **Verbal:** Does he like to talk about and discuss books?
3. **Aural:** Does she like listening to lectures, and books in electronic format, computers, e-books, etc.?
4. **Musical/Physical:** Is he musically inclined in singing, playing instruments, or dancing?
5. **Artistic:** Does she understand abstract concepts, like drawing/painting or working with puzzles/patterns?
6. **Tactile/Nature:** Does he like to hold books, or do hands-on activities, being outdoors and using natural materials?
7. **Logical:** Does she like to create computer games, solve problems, or do Math?
8. **Interpersonal:** Does he like socializing, groups, Facebook?
9. **Intrapersonal:** Is the student shy, quiet, or prefers to work alone?

Frequently, tutors will find that students have a variety of learning styles and interests that can be integrated into creating effective lessons.

Visual learners like colorful materials and pictures that they can associate information with in their minds. They also may like working interpersonally in groups, talking, and socializing with their peers. Another activity is using finger paints to make words and phrases, or labelling photographs with words.

Auditory learners learn mainly by hearing the spoken word. They may like to listen to lectures, books on tapes or CDs, and information contained in aural songs or poetry. They may like working in groups if the groups are attentive to the aural lesson. These types of learners may also be musically inclined, and learn to play music by 'ear,' simply because they have a keen focus on sounds. I record books and lectures using Audacity, an internet recording program, for my son-in-law who learns by listening to spoken information. He loves books on CDs or podcasts that he can listen to in his car. He reads when he has to, but he is bored by books in print. He routinely reads out loud to hear the information, so that he can remember it.

The logical learning style type of student may like lessons that provide step-by-step sequences to get the outcome. The shy student may prefer to work on a lesson at her own pace before asking for help. Students can have a variety of learning styles, so it is important that tutors have a variety of activities that are of interest to their students. Reading can be incorporated in having students decipher each lesson's instructions and objectives, no matter which learning style is involved.

Key #5 - Learn the Alphabet in Order and Randomly

There are twenty-six letters in the English alphabet that appear as uppercase and lowercase symbols. It doesn't matter which form the pair of letters are in (either uppercase or lowercase); they will make the same sound.

Use ABC songs and books; I sang a version of the ABC song to my grandchildren as a lullaby!

```
Left>                                    right
Aa Bb Cc Dd Ee Ff Gg
Hh Ii Jj Kk Ll Mm Nn
Oo Pp Qq Rr Ss Tt Uu
Vv Ww Xx Yy Zz
```

In order to help my grandson with letter recognition, my daughter lined the hallway with letters at his two-year-old eye level. She then taught my grandson to look for the letters that she called out, randomly as well as in order.

Learning to read begins with learning the letters of the alphabet. There are 26 uppercase letters and 26 lowercase letters. Some letters have circles, legs and tails that students need to recognize.

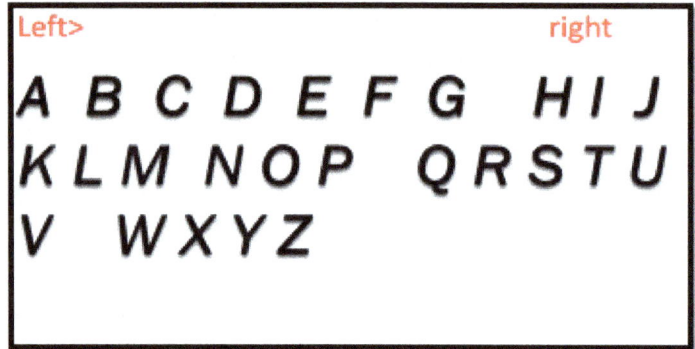

Key #5 - Learn the Alphabet in Order and Randomly

What do you see? Which group of letters is upside down?

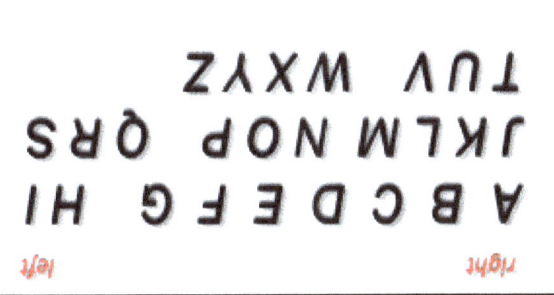

BDUEZFHAJLSMPNOQCRTV WKXIYG

Are the letters in random order or backwards?

ZYXW VU TSRQ PONMLKJIHGFEDCBA

Key #6 - Students Must Associate Sounds with Letters

Teach students to breathe the first **sound** of each letter. "Say this letter makes the 'aaa' sound." (I intentionally chose pictures of words that have the 'short' sound of the first vowel).

Teach students to breathe the first **sound** of each letter. "Say this letter makes the 'juh' sound."

Key #6 - Students Must Associate Sounds with Letters

Teach students to breathe the first **sound** of each letter. "Say this letter makes the 'sss' sound."

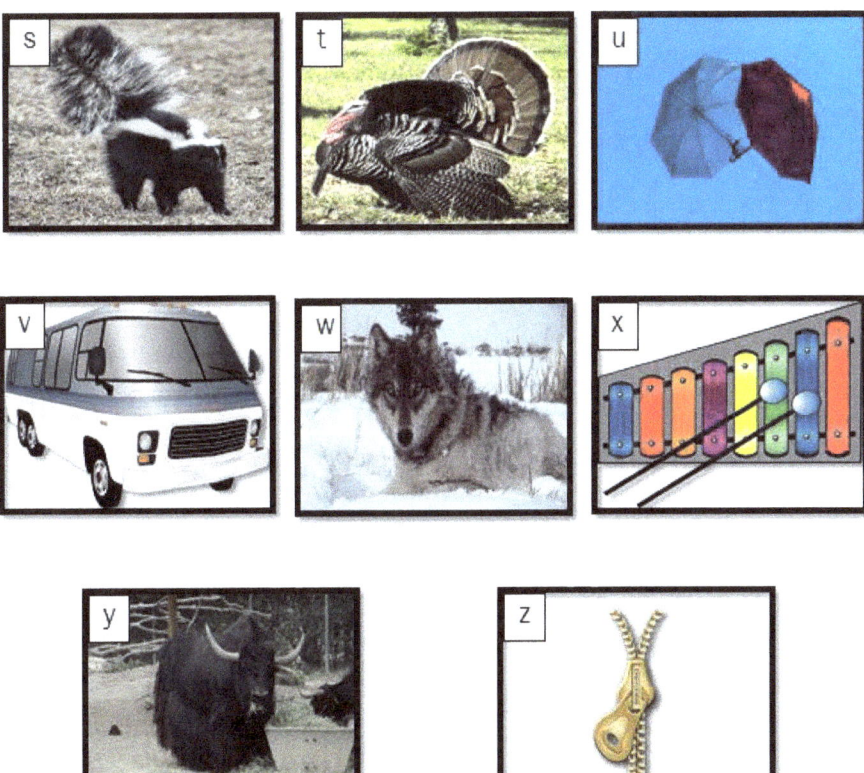

Key #7 - Learn Consonant Blends and Vowels

Vowels: a e i o u (and sometimes y)

It is easier to decode words if blended consonants and vowels are used together. The beginning sound in a word is called an onset, and the ending sound is called a rime (as you will learn in Key #9). Blip, clip, drip, flip and slip are good examples of using blend onsets and the –ip rime to create words. The old "Name Game" song, banana-fana-bodana-fee-fy-mo-dana lyrics are a great example of using rime endings.

Blends:

- BL   CL FL   GL   PL   SL
- BR   CR DR FR   GR   PR   TR   WR
- CH   PH SH   TH   WH
- SC   SK   SM   SN   SP   SQ   ST   SW
- SCH   SCR   SHR   SPL   SPR   SQU STR   THR
- And of course: ck dw kn gh   gn (sometimes letters are silent).

Key #8 - Learn to Hear Short Vowel Sounds First

I think the difference in the sounds is easier to understand, if students learn the basic short vowel sounds first. Some of the vowels have a variety of sounds because English is made of words from other languages such as French, Spanish, Latin, and British English.

There are over 60 rules for learning to pronounce English words, and practicing the short sound of the vowels helps students gain the initial confidence needed to tackle this language. You can find the various rules for pronunciations in any phonics book at your local library. I like to use names like Al or Alice, Essie or Bess, Mick, Olive or Rob, Bud, and Yvette to help students remember *short* vowel sounds.

Vowels: a   e   i   o   u   (and sometimes y)

Short vowel sounds

a - aaa apple   Al, Alice
e - eh   egg   B*e*ss, *E*ssie
i - iii igloo   M*i*ck
o - ow   owl   R*o*b, *O*live
u - uh   umbrella B*u*d
y -   g*y*m (y acts as a vowel when it is the only vowel in the word.) *Y*vette

Key #9 - Use PVC Phone Tool When Teaching Sounds

There are two things that I really like about the PVC Pipe Phone: (1) it's inexpensive to make, and (2) the ends are twistable, so tutors can actually speak into the phone as the student listens. This a great way to help students who have foreign accents understand the difference in letter sounds.

To build your own PVC pipe phone, you can buy a half inch diameter PVC pipe at a plumbing or hardware store and have a worker cut it into 15 three and a half inch pieces. Then buy two ¾" elbows to fit the ends of each piece to create a PVC Pipe Phone. This tool enables students to hear what they are saying. The PVC-Phone is especially helpful in listening to the short sounds of the vowels, especially the "aaa" and "eh" sounds.

The beginning sound of a word is called an "onset," and the ending sound of a word is known as the "rime." Using a single letter (usually a consonant), or a 2- to 3- letter blend at the onset of a word rime can help the student learn to make new words just by changing the sounds.

This technique is very helpful when building vocabulary, and engaging the student in fully understanding the relationship between letters and sounds. Students can then change "bat" into "cat," and *fat, hat, mat, pat,* etc. just by changing the onset. Similarly, students can change the rime of "cat" to make "can," or *cab, cob, cod, cub,* etc… You can mix up the onsets and rimes to make various new words: *bat, bed, red, hat, hit, sit, had, hot, not, mug, chug, big,* etc.

Generally, using onsets and rimes together in various ways is known as creating word families when the endings of the words actually rhyme or sound the same. Students gain confidence in their reading abilities as they add more words to their vocabularies.

Key #10 - Learn to Hear Long Vowel Sounds Last

The long vowel sounds are simply the sounds heard when one says the name of the letter: A says "ay!" B says "bee!" This is the easiest of all the rules to remember! I like to use names like April, Eli, Inez, Otis, Ulysses and Wyatt to help students remember long vowel sounds.

Vowels: a e i o u (and sometimes y)

Long vowel sounds

  a - A Apron April
  e - E Eagle Eli
  i - I Ice   Inez
  o - O Open Otis
  u - U Unicorn Ulysses
  y - sky (y has long vowel sound sometimes; and before silent e.) **Wyatt**

During this time students will be introduced to digraphs (two vowels together) and other interesting rules about vowels such as: the Silent E rule, and the R-controlled vowel rule. Remember to borrow library books about phonics to gain access to the various rules. Many literacy council lesson books for tutors also include these rules in the appendices. The children's television show, *Word World*, uses many of the rules in songs during each episode.

Key #11 - Learn Sight and Glue Words

I believe in the concept of teaching the whole brain to associate sounds, words, and pictures together. When a student struggles to put sounds together, it takes all of the energy out of trying to read (and some students forget what they are trying to do!). There are at a minimum 150 to 220 words on the common sight word lists. Many researchers agree that eighty percent of most reading material is made of sight words. This is also why it is important for students to learn by sight the words that hold and glue sentences together.

It is also a good idea to use audiovisual clips of words being highlighted in sentences as they are spoken. Examples of this type of highlighting can be found in children's educational programs like, 'Between the Lions' and 'Super Why' as stories are being read on camera or television. Other internet websites, like YouTube, News for You, and Interactive Weebly, also have video clips of highlighted words.

Children learn to recognize the symbols for fast-food restaurants and stores because their brains are looking for recognizable shapes and colors. My grandson called the What-A-Burger hamburger place the "golden triangle" before he could read because he recognized the neon-lit triangle on the front of each building. After we spent an evening searching fruitlessly for the "golden triangle" place (with a screaming two-year-old in the backseat of the car), we decided to start pointing out and pronouncing words to match the pictures that he was seeing!

I like using pictures to convey meaning of words, and I point to the beginning and ending letters to stress the beginning and ending sounds of each word.

| A after all am an and any are as ask |
| be because become before being but by |
| can came cold come **could** cry did do does |
| done each end every eyes few first for from |
| get give God good got |

| had has have *he* help *her* here **hers** *him* |
| *his* hot **how** *I* if in into is it just |
| knew know like look last large least left |
| made many may *me* *might* *more* most |
| *must* **my** new no none nor not now |

Key #11 - Learn Sight and Glue Words

of off old on one or our out own put

right said saw say see she should since

so some such than that the them then

there these they this thorough those though

thought through to too try

---

until upon use very want was water way

we well went what when where while

who whole why will with work would

yes yet you young your yours

Key #12 - Learn to Associate Mental Pictures with Words

You can also use **pictures** to teach abstract words, like: *to, of, a, the, a piece of cake; to the school...* Books by Dr. Seuss are great for rhyming, blending, and discussing the pictures one sees in the mind. You want to teach the student to see the picture associated with the sound in her mind. You can use rebuses, which are tiny pictures, in place of key words in a sentence to make sentences graphic and easier to understand, initially. Many public libraries have books in the rebus format that you can borrow. The rebus format is also used in a lot of primary math books to teach currency and other concepts. Money amounts are replaced with pictures of dollar bills or coins. Numeral symbols are also replaced with pictures of objects like cookies, jellybeans, apples, etc., to teach the operations of addition, subtraction, multiplication and division to students.

One can also use pictures to teach **Word Families**...if you teach *pig*, show a picture of a big pig and a small pig. Also, teach: *big, dig, fig, rig, twig, and wig*... (Use the 2-3 letter consonant blends to add vocabulary words). Students love being able to create words, and guess or match pictures to words!

This technique is very helpful when building vocabulary, and engaging the student in fully understanding the relationship between alphabets and sounds. Students can then change "bat" into "cat," and *fat, hat, mat, pat,* etc. just by changing the onset. Similarly, students can change the rime of "cat" to make "can," or *cab, cob, cod, cub,* etc…You can mix up the onsets and rimes to make various new words: *bat, bed, red, hat, hit, sit, had, hot, not, mug, chug, big,* etc. Just remember to use pictures whenever possible to do so.

Key #13 - Keep Learning Fun with Positive Reinforcement

Students like seeing their names in print, so I had my student print and use his name in a sentence on lined paper. Then we cut the sentence into separate words to create puzzle pieces. The sentence was something like: "John can read well." The sentence can be rearranged into: "Can John read well?" The sentence can be modified by changing the name/subject, action/verb, and/or adding objects to the end of the sentence. This is a great way to learn new vocabulary words, add movement to the lesson, and give the student more control over what he is learning. It's also the perfect time to discuss different forms of punctuation.

When you are creating positive sentences make sure you model the answer of "yes!" for your student. Say out loud, "Yes, you can read books well!" Praise and positive reinforcement builds confidence during the learning to read process. I love seeing enthusiasm and sparkling eyes on the faces of students who are gaining confidence in learning to read!

You are restoring the lost time and preparation for learning to read that many students didn't receive, individually. You are boosting confidence, and letting students know it is safe to relax, make mistakes, and enjoy the process of learning to read. Give the student time to mentally process the activity and make self-corrections. Ask questions like: "What do you think is happening in the pictures? What do you think will happen next? Does that make sense?"

During this time, you want to use the students' learning style as much as possible as you teach reading skills. Relaxed learners are able to gain reading skills quicker and better to become life-long readers.

Key #14 - Guide Thinking Before, During and After Reading

Tutors Should Model Questions, Students Should Think About Before, During, And After Reading By Asking: Why, When, Where, What, Who And How?

Tutors should model asking questions aloud about the material they and their students are studying. Who-What-When-Where-Why and How? are the details of a story or book being relayed to the reader. These questions promote critical thinking and help students to understand what they are reading.

I always want to know what *my student is really thinking* about the problem he or she is having when trying to read. Well, there is an AWESOME website called 'Reading Rockets' that addresses this issue. I love the Rocket Learns to Read book, but I didn't know there is also a website: http://www.readingrockets.org/helping/target. "Target the Problem" is only one of many tools on this website. I chose this one because it asks and answers questions from a student's, teacher's, and parent's point of view in all the areas of reading: word decoding, fluency, reading comprehension, sound awareness, vocabulary, etc. This is an awesome helping tool for understanding reading difficulties in students of ANY AGE!

Please also review the "Other Sources of Difficulties" for strategies and help in working with English Speakers of Other Languages, ADHD, brain processing, and combinations of issues with reading. It is important to reach students who have difficulty reading in grades four and higher to keep them from falling behind in the school system. There are middle school and high school students who are hiding their lack of reading abilities.

Students who struggle to read, especially students who stutter, may benefit greatly from the material on the Reading Rockets website. Tutors want to show a great deal of compassion and patience in their body language, non-verbal and verbal responses to these students.

Some of the most common questions that I receive from tutors pertain to getting students to remember what they've read in the previous lessons. It is easier to get students to remember reading something that they find interesting. These supplementary materials can be about a student's hobby, job, school, children, or something of personal significance.

It is important to discuss something about the reading materials to get the student thinking in that area. Tutors can use pictures or book covers to start the conversation. You may want to have several books with interesting covers about different subjects available from which to choose. Ask the student "What do you think this book is about? Why?" Learning to think critically begins when students look at the cover and title of a book.

Using that information they should try to determine what the book or story is about. It is a good idea to point to the pictures or words on the cover to ask "Where?" or "Who?" and "When?" As you read together it is important to ask these questions often to get the student to improve their understanding of events as they develop throughout the story. It is important to link understanding (reading comprehension) with the process of learning to read in the early stages. These same questions will be asked later on when students learn to write essays and take Language Arts comprehension tests.

Key #15 - Incorporate Capitalization and Punctuation

Students Should be Taught to Use Proper Capitalization and Punctuation During Reading Lessons

In teaching the balanced concept of reading, it is important to teach students to use capitalization and punctuation, early in the process. Tutors should point out that sentences start with capital letters, and end with punctuation marks.

Tutors should always use proper capitalization and punctuation when writing sentences from the beginning to get students accustomed to seeing and using these things daily. The easiest way to do this is to create sentences using the student's name, or the name of a city.

The second easiest rule of reading is that "Sentences begin with capital letters and end with some form of punctuation." When my daughter was young, she used to read out loud in long run-on sentences. She'd read as if there wasn't any punctuation in the selection. To get her pause and take a breath at commas, and stop at the end of sentences I became a drama queen. I'd raise my hands in the air and scream "Oh!!!! You've just killed me because you ran over me without stopping!" Then we'd both laugh because it was hilarious! She learned to look for, pause for, and stop for punctuation.

This is a great time to discuss the rules of proper structure, and the good grammar. Discuss how subjects (nouns and pronouns), verbs (action words), descriptive words (adjectives), etc. go together to create dynamic sentences and stories. Tutors want to continue to add more balanced knowledge as they build students' reading, writing, and critical thinking skills.

Key #16 - Build on Prior Knowledge and Life Experiences

Stories and Writing Should Build on Students' Prior Knowledge and Life Experiences to be Meaningful

As mentioned earlier, lessons should be centered upon things that are of interest and importance to students. In order to make sense of the concepts of reading, students need to be engaged in the lesson.

I helped teach my two grandchildren how to read. My grandson, Jonathan, had the full attention of three adults until he was almost three and a half when his sister, Zyonne, was born. We used to sing the "ABCs" song to Jonathan as a lullaby to calm his colicky crying spells. In our family, we joked that Jonathan would fall asleep when he learned to sing the ABCs in Kindergarten. I'd also let him "help" me to check my email at the computer by guiding his three-month old hands to click buttons on the keyboard.

When he was two or three we'd watch children television shows like, 'Word World', 'Super Why', 'Sesame Street', and 'Between the Lions' so that I could pause the show whenever highlighted words or phrases of a story appeared. The DVR is a wonderful tool for using cable to teach anyone to read! Those shows would routinely ask questions of the television audience, so I'd stop the screen of the show in order to give Jonathan plenty of time to make a choice. He'd have time to correct his choice, if necessary, and receive lots of praise for his efforts.

Jonathan got to practice his reading skills on trips to the grocery store. In the car as we passed by, I would ask him to tell me any words he knew on billboards, street signs, and business signs. He called out words like: zoo, no trucks, speed limit, McDonalds, Burger King, and What-a-Burger. Of course he had learned to recognize all of the fast food restaurant advertisements by the time he was three!

One day while waiting at the drive-through window of a What-A-Burger restaurant, Jonathan announces from his car-seat in the back of my car, "Grammy, the sign says 'Now is a good time to get a cookie!" I hadn't noticed that sign, and he was right, so I bought and gave a cookie to him! He was three and a half years old!

We practiced reading the overhead aisle signs in grocery stores to find the correct location for foods, and then he would have to find the right brand on the shelves. He thought it was the best game in the world to go shopping for groceries!

Jonathan got so much practice learning to read that he amazed the Kindergarten teacher during his entrance testing to the school. She had placed about ten different crayons before him and asked him to tell her the colors of each one. He wasn't sure about the purple crayon, so he picked it up and rotated it to read "violet" from the label out loud to her.

Zyonne, however, is learning to read at a more natural pace because the attention has to be shared with her brother. She loves books as much as her brother does, and she is still one of the top readers in her kindergarten class. Why? Zyonne loves calling out letters to spell words. She loves to practice reading the ten or more interesting library books in the backseat of my car. She and Jonathan will choose a story to read to me while I'm driving them to school, and sometimes I will finish reading the story to them in the school's parking lot.

Tutors should ask questions to find out what students understand about the information that is being discussed. Does the student have

Key #16 - Build on Prior Knowledge and Life Experiences

prior knowledge about the geographical area, working knowledge about the employment area, or does the student want to know more about the information? Would the student like to share information about his previous life experiences?

What interests and expertise does the student have? What are his hobbies? Does she have any unusual talents? Is he an artist or a gardener? What are her goals in the near future, and in five years? Is there something that he has always wanted to do? Not only do we want students to read to understand, but we also want them to enjoy the process of learning to read for the rest of their lives!

Tutors should find materials to make lessons on reading interesting and meaningful to students. Also, invite students to bring things that are of personal interest to the reading sessions. As you work together, teach students how to compose their thoughts into colorful essays as they write about their activities, families, jobs, etc. These essays can be simple and short, or long and complex and kept in a folder or journal. The purpose of writing is two-fold: (1) build on the student's knowledge and experiences, and (2) the student learns associate words and reading with events in his life.

When we ask adult students why they want to learn to read better, we get a lot of interesting answers, such as: to get a driver's license, to help my children with homework, to read the Bible, to read the letters my children wrote to me, etc...

Key #17 - Using Repetition and Summarization

Use Repetition, Comprehension Questions, and Summarization to Scaffold and Assess Student Understanding

It is okay to re-read books and articles; this practice is called scaffolding and repetition. It helps students become familiar with vocabulary words, sentence structure, proper grammar, and punctuation marks.

Repetition of a favorite story is also a good time for a tutor to ask a student to summarize the tale in their own words. Ask the 5W/1H questions: Who? What? Where? When? Why? And How? Tutors should ask questions to get students to think critically about what they are reading, and help students use the same questioning techniques when writing essays and stories.

Ask the student to think of a different ending or beginning for a story or article. This allows students to become creative, and assess their own understanding of the reading material. It also gives tutors opportunities to assess students' comprehension of the lesson, and change or correct misunderstandings.

Refer to the different punctuation symbols in the reading selection, and ask the student what each means, or provide an explanation. You want to model why sentences and passages should make sense to the reader. This is also a way to teach self-correction while reading to students.

Key #18 - Writing Starter: Incomplete Stories and Pictures

Use Action Pictures and Incomplete Stories as Writing Starters

Unusual pictures are a good way to get students to think critically. One can ask, Who? What? Where? Why? When? And How? questions to create stories and writing activities. Pictures really are worth a thousand words, and very helpful in building vocabulary.

Tutors can read most of a story to students, and have the students write a suitable ending, or change the ending of the story.

Really, officer, I have my driver's license. I got it in training school.

A treehouse is a great place to hang out with my friends!

Really... I want to be your friend. The stories I could tell you about living in this zoo!

If giraffes could talk, what do you think these giraffes would say?

Meet me at the watering hole before noon...

Key #18 - Writing Starter: Incomplete Stories and Pictures

I'm the big bear on the block, and I know where the best salmon are!

I'm just hanging around waiting for the mailman to come.

Music is my life! I'm just saying... Elvis's "I Ain't Nothing But A Hound Dog" rocks!

Key #19 - Oral Reading is Necessary to Build Fluency

Tutors want to help students learn to read aloud by using shared reading to model the process. It is important for students to hear themselves speaking words, phrases, and sentences. Oral reading enables tutors to hear students use proper pronunciation of vowels, blends, words and phrases.

Students can hear themselves speak and self-regulate their understanding of what they are reading. They can ask themselves if what they are reading and hearing makes sense. If the student stumbles over a word, or finds that something in the sentence does not make sense; he has the chance to self-correct what he is saying.

Does the student stutter when reading? Has the student been tested by a speech therapist? Does the student stutter when holding a regular conversation? If the student only stutters while reading aloud, he or she may be going too fast, be uncomfortable, or have some other issue. I used to stumble over words while reading aloud only in my eighth grade Social Studies class. I thought that the teacher was staring at me waiting for me to stumble! I didn't stutter in any other teacher's class… hmmm…

Have the student read the selection silently several times; then have the student read the selection aloud (and possibly into a recording device to hear himself). Stuttering /stumbling should decrease as the student becomes familiar with the material and builds self-confidence.

Key #20 - Teach Comprehension, Spelling and Writing

Students Can Learn to Comprehend, Spell and Write, Simultaneously as They Learn to Read

To gain meaning from passages, as one learns to read, write and spell words, is part of balanced information and reading fluently. Tutors can ask questions of students, and provide relevant explanations to assess the students' comprehension of the lesson.

Asking students to read, write and spell words as you question their understanding also helps build new memory associations in the brain. Incorporating word and sentence games in the lesson helps keep the student engaged in the learning process.

For example, *"The wolf ran home to make chicken stew in his kitchen." What did the wolf do? Can you spell "wolf," or "kitchen?" Where did the wolf go? Can you write the name of the recipe? Does this sentence make sense, or is it true? Can wolves cook?*

Tutors should take the time to build students' confidence and critical thinking skills as they focus on a new word or two or an old story. I believe the more students understand what they are reading, the more they will put into their long-term memories.

Ultimately, tutors want to teach students to write from the first lesson, so that writing and spelling becomes associated with the art of reading. Writing and spelling reinforces the view of alphabets and words in the brain for long-term memory.

Writing practice helps students to build vocabulary, word and picture association, and reading fluency. Always ask students to discuss with you what they have written. It is easier to pronounce and read words and phrases that one has used in writing stories and essays. It is important to practice writing, daily, so that it becomes easier in future lessons.

Most students will be familiar with printed text as that is what they will see most often in books. Teach students how to create printed letters, initially, and as the student improves charge ahead to teach cursive writing. Famous government documents like the Declaration of Independence and the Constitution of the United States are written in flowing cursive hand writing. Let's honor our forefathers and keep cursive writing alive! There are books and videos about how to write in the cursive style on YouTube.

To improve spelling, one has to see it...say it...write it...spell it...while looking at the words and without looking at the words; it takes practice, practice and more practice. The Scholastic Dictionary of Spelling by Marvin Terban, is a great book that has commonly miss-spelled words included, and can be found at most public libraries. A list of commonly misspelled words along with their correct spellings is also included at the back of this book. This is a great tool to guide tutors in teaching reading, spelling, and finding words in the dictionary.

READ! *A How-To-Guide for Tutors and Parents* will enable tutors to teach adults and children basic reading, spelling and writing skills from the beginning. I've also included a list of games that can be used to make learning to read fun during these lessons.

Learning Difficulties: Dyslexia, Dyscalculia, and Dysgraphia

In the introduction I noted that children and adults who have trouble reading might not have received guided instruction in how to read when they were younger. They may also struggle with some form of learning disability or dyslexia (including dyscalculia and dysgraphia).

The dictionary defines *dyslexia* as a reading disorder. *Dyscalculia* is defined as the inability to solve simple math problems. *Dysgraphia* is defined as the inability to write. Researchers are unable to agree on exactly what dyslexia is, and to what degree it is considered difficult. I believe that most of us have some form of dyslexia, dyscalculia, or dysgraphia. But I also believe that with help these learning disorders can be overcome in many cases. This is why it is so important to discover and teach to each student's learning style. It is equally important to "target the problem" to find what the student understands, and the problem he is experiencing.

Adults might not have learned to read for a variety of reasons ranging from physical impairment to lack of proper training to poor self-esteem.

Physical impairment… For the past year and a half I have been reading everything I can find about dyslexia. The simple definition is that dyslexia is a reading disorder affected by impaired vision and hearing. There are degrees of dyslexia from mild to severe, and experts cannot agree on what causes the condition. Some people have impaired eyesight that can be corrected with prescription eyewear; and hearing trouble that can be corrected with auditory devices. Some experts like to quip that dyslexia occurs in an area in the brain where the "wires are crossed," yet, many dyslexics are gifted in other areas, such as, mathematics, music, dancing, sports, and public speaking. There are a lot of famous people who had learning difficulties: Whoopi Goldberg, Charles Schwab, Andrew Carnegie, Ben Carson, Albert Einstein, Jim Carrey, Danny Glover, Steven Spielberg, Mohammed Ali, Henry Winkler, and others.

Teachers and others in society need to be trained to check for dyslexic symptoms so, that the problem can be arrested early to prevent a lifetime of avoidable misery. A quote attributed to Abraham Lincoln: *"Teach the children so it will not be necessary to teach the adults."*

Poor self-esteem... Children who suffer with dyslexia or apparent difficulty learning to read learn early in life how to hide the problem. Feelings of embarrassment, isolation, being left behind their peers, and anger can manifest into poor self-esteem and defeatism. Why is it so easy for others to read and yet I can't. What is wrong with me? They think they are different, dumb, yet they have other strengths and talents. And they are brilliant at coping with the problem of dyslexia and hiding it from everyone... including teachers...for years! They create different excuses to get out of reading/writing assignments or tasks: skipping school, losing assignments, acting out or becoming the class clown, pretending to be sick, etc. Eventually they may give up on learning how to read because it is just too painful of a process. They've learned to hide the reading difficulty so well that they grow up to become illiterate adults that will come to a literacy council for help, one day. Hopefully.

Lack of training.... Some of the adults we tutor in basic reading have never been trained to read from the left to the right side of words, sentences and pages. They haven't been taught that in the English language, we also read from the top of the page to the bottom. Children should have had years to absorb the mechanics of reading as they were read to before they entered kindergarten. Adults who did not receive structured training, or who weren't ready for formalized schooling sometimes get left behind their peers when it comes to learning to read. How can you see the difference, or hear the difference between letters and sounds, when you have never been taught to do so? And if one is learning to read English as a second language, there may be more difficulties.

Other languages may have a different arrangement than English, which can cause a lot of confusion in learning to read. (The Hebrew language is read from the opposite side of the book as compared to English. Sentences are read from the RIGHT to the left in Hebrew. Descriptive phrases and adjectives come after the subject in Spanish, which can lead to more confusion. "My mother's house" would be translated into "house of my mother" or "casa de mi madre" in Spanish…) English also uses alphanumeric characters, where other languages may use Arabic, Chinese, Japanese, Hebraic, and other symbolic characters.

An American public school teacher with 20+ students per class does not have the time to correct each student's learning problem. Hopefully, the teacher will recognize and alert the proper team that there is a problem so that the student will receive help. However, I have talked with a few adults who were too ashamed to admit they had problems reading while in school. They hid the problem from others, and became high school graduates who could not read!

As tutors we want to take all of these things into consideration as we work one on one to make friends, earn trust, and help students get the training they need to succeed in learning to read, or read better. Be a compassionate, positive influence in your student's life. It takes a great deal of courage to admit that one cannot read, or has trouble reading. Yet, today, there is more help available than ever before to correct reading problems. Some resources are listed on the Tutor Resources portion of the Anne Arundel County Literacy Council's website at ICANREAD.org.

I suggest you take the Dyslexia test on the following link, you may find that you have a form of dyslexia or not: http://www.dyslexicadvantage.org/dyslexia-test/ You will gain some insight into questions to ask students about the problems they are experiencing in learning to read, better.

It takes practice, relevancy, and association to get students to learn and remember concepts. I like using games to increase the fun level when teaching skills to make it memorable and meaningful! How do you make learning to write memorable...? Have you ever written with a wet sponge on a chalkboard? Have you ever written using finger paints as your pen? Have you ever recited your math times tables facts as you skipped rope? Have you tried to read pages upside down or backwards? Have you tried to create new words out of a long word, or used word ladders to climb to a new clue?

What does your student see, hear, and think when she reads? Has she been taught to view words, phrases and sentences from the left to the right sides, and top to bottom of pages? Do the words seem to move or float off the page? Sometimes using transparent overlays in different colors or printing pages on different colored background paper will anchor words in place. It is also important to have the student's eyes and ears checked for visual and hearing impairment to get corrective devices as needed.

Does the student ask Who? What? When? Where? Why? How? questions to see if what he is reading makes sense and is understandable? Does the student have trouble with writing and doing simple math problems? Has the student been shown how to hold a pen or pencil, properly, and how to create each letter of the alphabet? Has the student been shown how to effectively add and subtract numbers and objects, so that the concept makes sense? Does the student know the order of operations for doing math problems? If so, *dysgraphia,* trouble writing, and *dyscalculia,* trouble with numerical mathematics, may be ruled out as physical problems.

Students who have increased their vocabularies, sight and glue words can begin to envision and write down words that relate to stories in their imagination. Tutors can help students learn to write better by using reading materials that are written in three levels: easy, less easy, and more complex to showcase the use of adjectives, adverbs and other sentence structure.

In a similar manner, students can overcome dyscalculia. Tutors should take the time to incorporate pictures in the mind to booster student understanding of the mathematical concept. Ask a student 'Can you see the boy holding three cookies in one hand, and four cookies in the other hand? If he eats two cookies how many does he have left?' Does that make sense? Have the student test the concept using his favorite cookies!

The Illustrated Elementary Math Dictionary by Kirsteen Rogers provides basic math concepts in a simplified manner. The tutor and the student can read and discuss the sections to get to the root of any problems the student may be having. This book helps to build a firm foundation in the meaning of numbers. I also suggest using grouping tools, such as abacus beads or lots of buttons, coins, and other objects to help students visualize number groupings in addition, subtraction, multiplication and division.

At the same time that you are showing students how to group numbers, see math pictures in their minds, you also want to put the numbers in words to relate the concepts to mathematical word problems. There is a myth that math word problems are hard because many of us don't understand what we are reading and what the question is asking.

If we have ruled out problems with vision by using corrective eyewear, we can begin to concentrate on physical reading and understanding numbers and seeing mathematical concepts in our minds. We can work with students' learning styles to provide videos, audio, colorful charts, magnetic numbers, and math games to enable students to learn in ways that are understandable to them.

Another book that I like using is <u>Elementary Algebra for College Students</u> by Allen R. Angel. Angel not only shows how to get problems right, but he also shows two or three ways students may have worked the problem incorrectly! He teaches the basic concepts of mathematics and provides excellent explanations in every section. I have given away more copies of his book than any other to students, and the positive feedback is amazing! Angel helps one to build a firm mathematical foundation to understanding numbers.

It is important that tutors model the proper way to read, write, and do math. One on one tutoring is an excellent way to get to the heart of the problem for individual student reading difficulties. Good readers are trained to read well!

Reading Tools and Games

In the last section of this book, I want to discuss how to use free learning resources to help teach students to read, spell and write, properly. There are hundreds of books; tools and rules; literacy websites; and games that can be used to promote reading. Teaching reading can be an inexpensive undertaking when one uses these items or creates one's own reading resources.

Word Families and Rhymes

Word Families are a way to associate words and arrange them in a group that makes sense. The words in each family abide by the same rules, either having the same or similar rimes (endings), sound, or having a similar function. For example, ball belongs to the *–ay* word family, but so does *day, hay, lay, say,* and *way*. They all sound alike because they all have the rime: -ay. Students can create new vocabulary words for the –ay word family by changing the onset (beginning sound) to a single letter or two to three letter blend, such as: *pay, ray, stay,* and *stray*. Most books about phonics have groups of sight-words listed in word families for short and long vowel sounds.

Dr. Seuss books are very popular with beginning readers because many of the sentences end in words that rhyme with the last word of a previous sentence. Nursery rhymes take advantage of the rhyming technique to make the lyrics easy to remember, too. We all remember popular *Mother Goose Tales*, like *Humpty Dumpty and Hickory Dickory Dock*, and children's songs like *Twinkle, Twinkle, Little Star and Old MacDonald* that use rhyming lyrics.

I encourage tutors to find and print out the lyrics to students' favorite poems or songs for use in a lesson. I learned to sing *Somewhere Over the Rainbow* by Judy Garland after listening to and reading the lyrics of the song on YouTube. The internet is a good source of rhyming poetry, songs, and audio clips, so that one can hear the sounds of the words.

Online Dictionaries and PVC Phones

Tutors should introduce students to online dictionaries and old-fashioned printed book dictionaries as soon as possible. Dictionaries are arranged in alphabetical order, so using the dictionary is a great skill to learn.

Online dictionaries are available on the internet for use in finding the definitions of words, and words with similar and opposite meanings. *Dictionary.com* is free, and it includes audio clips that one can use to hear the sound and syllables of the selected words. I sometimes input words that I might be unsure of the meaning into dictionary.com to get correct meaning while I am reading a novel. I can also click on the audio icon adjacent to the word to hear its pronunciation, and I find this action helps me to remember the word.

The PVC Phone is a manual tool for hearing sounds better. It is constructed from PVC pipes into the shape of a telephone receiver, so that the student speaks into one end and immediately hears her voice as the phone is held to her mouth and ear. One can purchase a half inch PVC pipe and have it cut into 3 and a half to 4 inch pieces at a hardware store. Then add ¾ inch elbow pieces to each end of a 4 inch section to create a phone. The phone enables students to really hear what they are saying. This is especially good for distinguishing between *short* vowel sounds of *aaa, eh, iii, ou,* and *uh.* There is a difference between *ape* and *app*…the first is a long sounding vowel and an animal, the other is a short sounding vowel and a computer application! Put the PVC Phone to your ear and practice saying your vowel sounds. And remember to teach the short vowel sounds, first!

Picture Words, Rebuses

The old saying, "A picture is worth a thousand words" really holds true when learning to read the English language. Tutors can use picture word cards to teach simple words and phrases. The picture of an apple can be used to teach "apple," or "green apple," or "worm in apple," or "**a** slice **of** apple." It all depends on what is depicted in the picture. Pictures are a great way to teach the preposition sight-words: **of, to, a, the**….etc.

When one uses a small picture in place of a word or phrase in a sentence, the picture is called a rebus. Rebuses help glue a sentence together, much like the sight-words, making reading easier. Public libraries have books in the rebus format that make reading fun. One of my favorites is <u>The Robin in the Tree</u>, by Dana Meachen Rau. There are six books about different animals in this rebus series.

Graphic Organizers and Pyramids

Any tool that draws the students' attention to a word, phrase, or sentence can be known as a graphic organizer. They vary in structure and design. A sheet of page with a tiny rectangle cut in it is a graphic organizer, so is a small slip of paper with a rectangle large enough to allow one to see a complete sentence. Write a sentence on a piece of paper; then cut that sentence strip into separate words… you have created a graphic organizer and a puzzle. Now, the student has to arrange the separated words into a sentence! They have to organize the words, and you can add punctuation marks to change the sentence from a statement to a question or exclamation. Graphic organizers can be used to focus on words or phrases or sentences to build vocabulary and reading comprehension. Have students use a dictionary to find and define any word they do not understand while that word is focused on in the organizer.

While focusing on words, another tool to use is the pyramid organizer. Draw a wide-bottom pyramid on a sheet of paper or a whiteboard. Build a sentence by adding a starting word at the top of the pyramid. Add one or two additional words as the pyramid gets wider until you reach the base with the entire sentence.

For example, let's use "The red fox jumps over the brown wall" in a pyramid:

The

The red

The red fox

The red fox jumps

The red fox jumps over

The red fox jumps over the

The red fox jumps over the brown

The red fox jumps over the brown wall.

Not only have we created a pyramid, but we have trained the eyes how to read from left to right and top to bottom to create a meaningful sentence. Use a ruler or piece of paper to cover the pyramid, and lower the cover from the top down to reveal each new line. Pyramids are a great way to add new vocabulary to reading material! Use the line from a student's favorite song or story to create a pyramid. If a student has trouble with the background colors of words, remember to use two different colored transparencies (yellow and blue, etc.) to help ease the blur strain on their eyes.

Shared Reading, Choral Reading

Sometimes struggling readers find it easier to read when the task is shared with the tutor or another student. I like finding an exciting story and having the student read a repetitious phrase as their part. The student gains confidence as they repeat the phrase in the story as their part of the reading session. Shared reading can also be used as the tutor reads a few sentences and then the student reads the next few sentences or passage. Tutors are modeling reading fluency for the student as the student listens and waits for their turn to read.

The same strategy can be used as tutors and students read together, simultaneously. Students need to practice reading out loud, so that they can hear themselves and gain confidence in reading fluently. Dr. Seuss' books are great for any type of reading; singular, shared, and choral. Some libraries have lists of books that are excellent for shared and choral reading strategies.

Create Student *Little* Books

As students learn more skills, you want them to keep copies of their work in folders. Creating little books out of favorite sentences, and poems or songs is also a good way to highlight what a student has learned. These books can be as simple as creating one for each letter of the alphabet, or blends, or phrases using sight words and construction paper. Students can also create more complex poetry or "spoken word" prose to write about today's social problems.

To focus on ownership, make sure students have a cover page with the title. Each student should add his name as the author (and illustrator if they created any sketches or pictures) of the book.

Word Ladders, Jokes and Riddles

Increase the fun level in your teaching sessions by including Word Ladders, jokes and riddles. I found books about Word Ladders in the public library. A picture of a ladder is displayed with clues and blank spaces about missing words at each rung. The beginning word is usually given and additional clues for how to change, add or subtract letters are given as students climb up the ladder. This is a great way to reinforce word meaning, spelling, and learn new vocabulary.

Another way to gain vocabulary is to use books of jokes and riddles in lessons. The punch lines of jokes and riddles are usually associated with a picture in the mind. The funny mental picture makes it easier to add vocabulary to long-term memory. One of my biology teachers created jokes about the course in his lectures, and the answers of many of his test questions were the punchlines!

Bingo, Quizzes and Puzzles

Word games such as BINGO in addition to quizzes and puzzles add a layer of fun to any lesson! Tutors can easily create segmented BINGO players' cards, and use flashcards of playing words and blends. Students can use buttons and bottle caps, etc. to mark the words that have been called during the game. Tutors and students can use the rules of the regular BINGO game, or create new rules to play.

Quizzes and puzzles are generated easily online, but can also be created, manually. There are many English Language Arts quiz and puzzle websites that have games for a variety of academic subjects. The moveable, colorful word pieces add memorable pathways in the brain as puzzles are solved. Students get hands-on kinetic experiences as they move words and pieces in the puzzles and games.

Reading Tools and Games

The *Many Things* website at http://www.manythings.org/ was developed to help English as a Second Language Speakers (ESL), but it is a great site for anyone trying to improve reading. You should check with the library's reference librarian to see if the computer has the required Flash software capability. (Some of the videos are also found on YouTube).

The *Many Things* site consists of vocabulary lessons, videos, quizzes and games. Additionally, some of the lessons allow students to listen along as the lesson is read. *Many Things* is a work in progress, as some of its resources are better than others. It may take time to load some of the programs, but the time spent on this website is valuable! There are Listen and Read Along video clips that show words being highlighted as they are read; there are lists of sight words and pages of related sentences; easy vocabulary games with pictures; and there are stories of various topics to interest most adults and motivate them to read (write and spell) more often.

Internet Websites with Audio Clips and Video News

Adult basic readers can gain confidence by using websites that have clickable embedded sound bites to help in hearing the correct pronunciation of words, phrases and sentences. Generally, an audio icon with an arrow is somewhere on the page to symbolize that one can listen to the word or passage. Audio clips are very useful for listening to new vocabulary or unknown words.

Audio and video clips with narratives are especially useful in listening to and reading news articles. Students can access the information on any electronic device, including smartphones, which make it easier to practice reading anywhere. At first glance, you might think the Interactive Sites for Education are only for children. Take a closer look at http://interactivesites.weebly.com/ and you will find something for everyone in the family! The topics include: Art, Brainteasers, English Language Arts, Holidays, Math, Music, Science, Social Studies, Spanish, Teacher Tools, and Typing.

I've tried a few of the games in the English Language Arts (ELA), Math, and Typing sites, and they are phenomenal! The ELA games help make learning every aspect of grammar fun. As a matter of fact, the games are so fun and inviting that my grandson begged to play a Multiplication game! We have been searching for something to help make learning Math less painful for us. He's nine and beginning the fourth grade, and had Math homework every night last year. This website helped eliminate his whining and procrastinating!

If a picture is worth a thousand words, then this site is valuable in the Language Arts games it provides to help students build proper sentences. The graphics are amazing and make learning interesting. I've tried several games: "Does it make sense?", "Kung-Fu Sentences", (ESL Do You Want to Be a Millionaire?), "What is in here?" puzzle pieces, "Who, How, Type, What, Where" building silly sentences… etc. These games are fun!!!!

The articles on the website, www.newsinlevels.com, are written in three levels which allow the sentences to show good examples of subject-verb agreement. The site has good examples of sentences and thoughts that range from simple (level 1) to complex (level 3). If so inclined, one can read the more complex statements of level 3, and then simplify them by reading level 1 to reveal the difference. Narratives accompany the audio-video clips for each level.

Google and YouTube also have wonderful videos to help with just about everything! Sometimes students need to do something, like move or dance to make a connection between letters, sounds, words, and comprehension. The instructors on YouTube are just as varied in their teaching styles and accents as students are in their learning styles! One

Phonics Rules

The <u>Scholastic Dictionary of Spelling</u> by Marvin Terban is only one of many books that have the rules and tricks to help in memorizing phonics of the English language. Remember the rhyme "i before e except after c?" …for words like believe, retrieve and deceive. Although there are exceptions, the expanded rhyme works even better: "i before e except after c, or when sounded like a, as in neighbor and weigh." (Terban, 1998, p.13) The book also lists word exceptions to the poem: ancient, being, scientist, weird… etc…I love the word **weird** because the 'i' comes after the 'e'….isn't that weird?!

Most public libraries carry books and materials about phonics, and generally, adult basic literacy training books have phonics rules in the appendices. The Laubach method is used by the Anne Arundel County Literacy Council because the <u>Laubach Way to Reading</u> books integrates phonics in each chapter lesson. Laubach's motto is "each one, teach one" as each tutor-student pair share a learning experience.

Incomplete Stories

Telling incomplete stories is a great way to get students interested and engaged in creating and writing the ending of stories. Students can create new endings for familiar stories. For instance, what might have happened if Rapunzel had escaped the tower by herself? Or supposed the three bears had been home when Goldilocks knocked on the door? Or maybe the storytellers got it wrong… can a turtle really outrun a rabbit?

Using incomplete stories to ask questions: Why? What? etc., can be great ways for students to begin thinking critically and write new stories. It builds reading comprehension as students are required to think about what is happening in stories. One has to understand what is going on before one can write a different ending, or perhaps a new beginning! One can also input the term "story starters" in Google to find websites that offer interesting sentences to use for this task.

Tutors want to make it easy for their students to use vivid imaginations as they create mental pictures of what is happening in stories. Writing the stories helps students to associate words with the pictures to add more vocabulary to their long-term memories. Remember reading, spelling, and writing all go together to build competent readers.

Moving Forward

Now that your student has learned the basics of reading, you want to continue to forge ahead to add more strength to her reading skills. Particularly, you want to encourage reading higher-level books to gain more vocabulary and comprehension knowledge. Public libraries in most states have lists of award-winning popular authors and illustrators of high interest books. The ultimate award is the Newbery Award for authors, and the Caldecott Award for illustrators. The state of Maryland has the Black-eyed Susan book lists for kindergarten through 12th grade readers. Florida has the Sunshine State Young Readers Awards. Ask your local librarians about the various book awards and available lists in your state.

It is also important to discuss the many rules of phonics because English is language of mosaics. The English language changes almost daily as new words and phrases are incorporated from recent immigrants to America. In order to discuss the relevant rules of phonics with which a new vocabulary word may be associated, look at how the short or long vowels or digraphs are used in the word and discuss words with similar vowel patterns and sounds. Have the student spell and write the word to aid in adding the word to long-term memory.

The next step to take after a student learns to read is to "read to learn." You want the student to read everything (from aisle signs in grocery stores to road signs on the streets and highways)! He should be reading and comprehending written instructions and directions. You are preparing him to complete homework assignments, job applications, college exams and standardized tests.

The way I've gotten better at taking timed tests is to practice a lot using a timer. If I know the test will be 30 minutes, I set the timer for

15-20 minutes. Then I practice taking a test with the same number of questions until I get more comfortable with the time I have. It helps to know that I have 1 to 3 minutes to answer each question. And one can skip questions on computerized tests, mark them for review, and come back at the end of the exam to answer them (time-permitting). The main thing is to practice taking tests and do the easy questions first.

Because the student has been having fun learning to read, he or she should be motivated to continue to do so. Tutors want to continue to push this momentum by having students study reading materials that hold relevancy to their futures, model how to compose essays, comprehend reading selections, and complete sentence organizers for grammar. Public libraries have novels that use highlighted Scholastic Aptitude Test (SAT) words in stories to improve students' Language Arts scores.

When the student is ready, have him select a novel to read and discuss with you. Libraries also have books that provide guided preparation techniques for all the major college and law school examinations: SAT, GED, GRE, LSAT, etc.

How to Get Rid of Test-taking Anxiety

The key to being calmer while taking tests is to prepare, prepare, prepare. To take a major test like the GED, SAT, GRE, LSAT, and high school standardized tests for the end of the school year; one has to practice to get control of the timing. There are preparation books and CDs and DVDs that are very useful for practicing strategies to understand the test language and answer questions.

I suggest that all students take six weeks to two months to study (at least one hour every other day) for a major exam on the state or national level. Take the pre-test first to find out what areas you need more help in, study those areas, and take practice tests. The test preparation books have helpful hints and strategies that tell you exactly what to do to rule out the obviously wrong answers and find the correct answers to questions, and to write beautiful essays. (And set a timer for 15 minutes less than the time given for each test when you practice).

One has to know what the test preparers and graders are looking for when one is taking tests. The terminology is very important! For instance, GED stands for General Equivalency Development or General Education Degree. To make it less intimidating, I renamed the Graduate Record Exam (GRE) (for graduate students that are studying for their Master's and Doctorates)… the "God Rocks Eternally" test! You have to keep your sense of humor while preparing and taking exams.

The five exams of the GED can be difficult: Writing Essay, Language Arts, Science, Social Studies and Math. The good news is that you don't have to take all five exams at the same time. In some states an essay is no longer required on the Social Studies exam, but students should be prepared to write one.

It is a good idea to use your library card to check-out several GED preparation books. You'll want to get the latest yearly version, if possible, to see what is required on the latest test. However, when it comes to writing an excellent essay, I suggest you borrow a book by Kaplan, Inc. from the Simon & Schuster publishers. I like the way the instructions and strategies are given in Kaplan books to prepare to write essays, analyze reading comprehension and English language grammar sections. Kaplan simplifies the writing process, and breaks down components into examples and answers, beautifully. Kaplan's "22 principles of effective writing" are explained, very well in the analytical writing section in several of their books.

I practiced creating essays using the Kaplan Test Prep and Admissions GRE Exam 2006 Edition: Comprehensive Program for about two months before I took the Graduate Record Exam. I love how this book explains the correct and incorrect ways of writing. Although the GRE exam is at a higher level its strategies can be used to pass the GED exam, too.

You'll want to compare this book to the strategies given in a more current GRE or GED preparation book. You can borrow the Cracking the GED Test 2016 by Geof Martz by the Princeton Review publishing house from your public library. GED books will teach you the strategies for understanding the reading sections of the test. This is important because the last two tests of the GED, Science and Social Studies, have a lot of reading. You can't really learn that material, but you have to be able to understand the type of questions you are given to be able to find the answers in the reading passages. It's easy once you know the techniques of how to do it!

You can also peruse tutor resources on your local literacy council's website. The ICANREAD.org website of the Anne Arundel County

Literacy Council has Tutor Resources and Library page for more GED resources, videos and games, and more. YouTube is also a great resource for anything that you want to know. In most cases, someone has asked the same question and made a video about the answer. I love YouTube videos!

Khan Academy is a really great website that has really great instructors and videos that can help teach you about basic Math and complex Math, like Algebra and Calculus. Another way to get a good foundation for basic Math would be to borrow Math DVDs from the local library. You can find out what your local library has without leaving your house just by checking your local library's website. I just checked the Anne Arundel County Public Library website, and there are a lot of basic math DVDs available for use.

My favorite Math DVD is by the comedy group: Standard Deviants… they are hilarious! My favorite Algebra book is: Elementary Algebra for College Students by Allen R. Angel. Angel builds a mathematical foundation as he begins with the basic numbers and number lines concepts.

Please review this interesting YouTube GED Math video: https://www.youtube.com/watch?v=J1njGBZe_Uk.

There will be Math and Statistics on the GED!
"Hey diddle diddle, the median's the middle;
You add and divide for the mean;
The mode is the one that appears the most,
And the range is the difference between."
Mean mode median. (n.d.). Retrieved July 01, 2016, from https://www.pinterest.com/able4cable/mean-mode-median/

I used the book: <u>Elementary Algebra for College Students (8th Edition)</u> by Allen R. Angel, Jan 13, 2010. He provides answers, lots of examples, and video references of how to do most of the math that you will be required to know on the GRE. There are ten chapters leading from basic number systems to Geometry to Quadratic and Linear equations. Angel shows how to get the right answers, and also how you got the WRONG answers! You can buy a used copy on Amazon.com, or borrow it from the public library. I gave my copy to a 9th grade student, and he loves it!

When studying for the GED or any exam, it is important to work on your Math at least three days a week, and to work on your reading/language arts/words/writing… every other day!!!!

All of these resources are free!

You can pass the GED, but you have to start studying and practicing the right way. It's important to find a good preparation book, and learn the test-taking strategies, as soon as possible. Remember the key to being calmer while taking tests is to prepare, prepare, prepare so that you know what to expect and what to do!

Churches, PTAs, Literacy Councils, and other groups may arrange speaking engagements via sarahkgardner@yahoo.com.

Note from the Author

I wrote READ! *A How-To-Guide for Tutors and Parents* as a practical tool for tutors and students to incorporate past and present methods of teaching reading into a balanced system. Phonemic awareness, phonics, comprehension, vocabulary, oral reading, fluency, spelling, and writing are all skills that are associated with the process of reading. Adults and children should have fun learning to read. I've included a list of reading tools and games to help keep lessons entertaining.

You can help build confidence in those who are struggling to read by using books that are easy (on the student's level) and those that are just a tad bit beyond the student's current reading level¬. Have the student read books that are easy in which he only makes one or two mistakes per page. If the student makes two or three mistakes per page, that book is considered a tad bit difficult which is perfect for increasing his/her vocabulary. If the student makes five mistakes or more on a page that book is too difficult. You do not want to frustrate the student by having him/her struggle needlessly while reading. Choose books that your student(s) are comfortable reading, and also choose interesting books to read to student(s). Everyone loves listening to a good story!

READ! *A How-To-Guide for Tutors and Parents* will enable tutors to teach adults and children basic reading skills. Students can learn to read easier as they learn to associate the letters, sounds, blends, sight words, and pictures to make meaning out of the English language. This is the first step adults can use to focus on the rules of reading, learning to write, and spelling as they practice daily.

And remember to spend lots of time with your students in or online at your local public library. Libraries have lots of free materials including e-books, electronic devices, games, and computer technology that promote literacy! We have evolved into the digital age as computers get so small we now wear them on our ears and wrists. We use Bluetooth technology in our cellphone earpieces and wristbands to stay connected to the world.

American public schools are promoting computer media as all grade-level students are being taught to create their own computer programs and applications. Using pre-generated blocks of code in graphical form, students learn to select, drag, and drop pieces to enable animated objects to move.

This software technique uses pictures, short phrases, and repetition to motivate students to create Minecraft, Star Wars, Angry Birds, Frozen, and other characters. Kindergarten students are learning to drag puzzle pieces into sequential order to build software and learn the art of animation. Websites like: Code.org and Scratch offer free platforms to teach computer coding. These sites might be of interest to adult students who have a visual, logical or physical style of learning. The Code.org website uses videos and helpful hints to teach computing strategies.

There are also lesson plans and scripts that explain the process of coding in great detail. Manipulatives (like printouts of diagrams and physical movement) are used in some lessons to engage students in understanding the algorithms of the lessons. There is one in which students physically fold paper to create an airplane that will fly! My grandchildren love standing up to emulate the movement of the steps they are creating to see if they should choose 'right' or 'left' to create geometrical figures.

If interested, students are also able to click on a button to show the actual programming language behind each block of code. This is helpful for older students who are considering becoming computer language programmers in the future. The kindergarten and older elementary students that I've worked with on the Code.org website enjoy the

Note from the Author

various lessons, and will easily spend an hour or more completing puzzles before their interest wanes!

Computer coding can be fun and an incentive for adults who want to learn something useful and lucrative as they learn to read! The repetitive short phrases of the visual blocks make it easier and more enjoyable as students to learn to read, make self-corrections, and create miniature computer applications.

A Typical Tutor's Question

A common question that I receive from tutors is how to get adult students to do their reading homework or practice reading more. My answer typically is that it would be very beneficial for your student to find something that he or she WANTS to read.

There are several questions you should ask about the student and his learning style. What does she like to do for fun? How does she learn best… dancing/moving, listening to music, walking to problem-solve, sitting, reading quietly, listening to lectures, or using hands-on activities, etc.?

It is important to find age-appropriate activities for each walk of life (toddler, children, teen-ager, young-adult, and adults including seniors) that pique the student's interests. What is he enthusiastic about? What are her interests? Does she like to cook or bake, sew or design clothes, crochet or knit, Zumba or spinning, lift weights, dieting and exercise, draw, paint or decoupage, visit museums, cathedrals or amusement parks, computer games, playing cards, or cleaning house? Is she employed or looking for employment? Is she interested in being promoted to the next level at work?

The library has pictorial books that have colorful pictures that outline the steps for many activities, like: cooking, baking, crocheting and sewing clothes. Ask a librarian for help to find them, or search by "tutorial." Is he active in church activities? Does she play an instrument? What is her favorite movie or television show, and has she read the biographies of the actors? The library has books written like screen-plays that follow the storyline of many of the latest movies, too.

If she could be whatever or do whatever she has always wanted to do… what would that be? Would she be an author, dancer, athlete, doctor, attorney, nurse, teacher, riverboat pilot, airplane pilot, cruise ship captain, 18-wheeler truck driver, movie star, missionary, auto-mechanic, software or computer engineer, or President of the United States of America? Would he invent the next best product to go viral on the internet or television? Would she be a television reporter, anchor person, game-show host, or a radio broadcaster? Would she start her own childcare business or some other business? Would he travel all around the world? Would she become a pastor or an accountant?

Find her interests then incorporate reading activities into her daily life so that you can discuss them as part of your lessons. There are books, CDs, DVDs, e-books and Play-Away systems that can be borrowed from the public library that can satisfy all these interests, and more!

The student can follow along in the book as he listens to it being read from an iPod, tablet or computer. The News-in-Levels website, http://www.newsinlevels.com, also has news articles with matching transcripts that adds more descriptive vocabulary in longer sentences in levels 1, 2, and 3. I also like using the YouTube website to find out how to do everything. Someone has done whatever you are looking for, and they have shared their results on YouTube. YouTube has great music, and video stories, tests, job descriptions, and teachers!

Ask your public librarians for old magazines they are about to discard to get interesting articles and pictures. I used to love the old Readers' Digests humor and daily word sections. Some of the jokes were hilarious! Suggest that your student keep a book, magazine or magazine clipping in every part of the house (including the bathroom and her pocket) for easy access to reading material (and read and change them each week). Your refrigerator door is also a good place to display articles.

Does she have a Smart phone on which she can play games and view the internet? Has she tried reading articles on her phone? Does she use a cell-phone or a computer constantly? Does he have an e-book reader, Kindle or Nook? Many of those devices have an Audio setting to hear the book being read as you follow the story on-screen.

Soooooooooooooooo.... What does your student like to do AND what is his learning style?

An Adult Student's Perspective

The following is an interview I did with Mr. M*; he gave permission to share his story with others. He wants you to know how important it is to take the time to work with people who may learn differently.

Mr. M testified in church about the struggles he had learning to read. He didn't learn as a child; in fact, he didn't learn until he had been in prison for ten years!

His story intrigued me. I had so many questions, but I didn't want to offend him or pry into his personal business. Yet, I wanted to know whether or not he had been affected by dyslexia… maybe he saw letters upside down and backwards…maybe the letters moved or fell off the page. I've read so much about the symptoms of dyslexia that addressed those issues recently.

One day, a prime opportunity presented itself when I saw Mr. M* in an area alone at church. I quietly asked him if he minded answering a few questions. He smiled and said I could ask him anything. We talked for the next twenty minutes as I asked about his reading issues and I was surprised at his responses!

He said he sees the regular alphabet, and hears the normal sounds, but… no one had ever encouraged him to learn to read properly. No one in his family and none of his teachers at school had ever taken the time to show or help him learn how to read. They labelled him "slow" or "dumb" and made fun of him and some of the teachers embarrassed him in front of his peers! He lost his sense of self-worth and self-esteem, so he became a trouble-maker in school. He was angry and fought everybody (including teachers).

That path led him to prison with no hope of parole. Then he met some positive role models in other prisoners who suggested he learn how to read. He thought to himself, "Why learn to read now? I'll never get out of prison." But after ten years and being urged by friends to learn to read, he decided to try again. He began to study and learn five words a day. When he started he had been incorrectly spelling three-letter words like "cat" as "kat." With the help of friends, he began to improve and he enrolled in the GED classes.

He met resistance from some of the prison's teachers who didn't like his outspokenness, so they tried to delay his progress by denying testing to him. But Mr. M said he prayed a lot and the Holy Spirit kept him trying and studying. He began to read law books and understand them! He really likes case studies and legal precedents! Mr. M persevered until he was allowed to take the GED exams and he passed them! And today he is also out of prison as well. God is good!

What I learned is that positive encouragement has value and is necessary to help all students want to learn. There are many ways to learn and encouragement is the first step in the process.

Mr. M* is only one of the reasons why it is really important that "Each one, teach one" in the Laubach way.

Annotated Book References

I have included an annotated list of book references in this section that tutors may find helpful. For further information, I suggest that tutors borrow books from public libraries through inter-library loan systems.

Angel, A. R., Petrie, D. R., & Semmler, R. (2000). Elementary algebra for college students. Upper Saddle River, N.J: Prentice Hall.

This book is a must-read, must-practice tool to use learning the concepts or real numbers, basic algebra, geometry, solving and understanding mathematical word problems. The author explains how to solve correctly, and also how a student might have gotten incorrect answers.

Anne Arundel County Literacy Council. I CAN READ.ORG website via www.ICANREAD.org

The AACLC website has a lot of free tutor resources and technology tips for aspiring tutors and students. There are links to webpages of resources about reading, writing, mathematics, English Speakers of Other Languages (ESOL), spelling, General Education Development (GED) materials, Citizenship, worksheets, games and other materials on this site.

Books, P. (2013). Reversing dyslexia: Improving learning & behavior without drugs.

Dr. Phyllis Books provides various insights and success stories into the world of dyslexia. There are many forms of Dyslexia that relate to having trouble learning to read, write, spell, calculate, listen, speak, concentrate, understand, sit still, and memorize, etc. There are numerous theories on what is considered Dyslexia and possible corrections.

Cook, A. (1999). How well does your child read, write, and do math?: Step-by-step methods for parents to assess and develop their child's skills. New York: Galahad Books.

Ann Cook has written a fabulous book to help anyone assess and train students to read, write, and do mathematics better. She has a section: *Grade Level Guidelines* on page 29 that teaches the basic to complex skills of Math for Kindergarten through fifth grades. I have been searching for ways to make learning Multiplication easier to help my 9-year-old grandson. This section works for him! He used the ten times tables, magical nines, and squares chart to practice. The charts are great because one can multiply the numbers either way very easily as one uses his fingers to intersect the rows and columns.

Fertig, B. (2009). Why can't U teach me 2 read?: Three students and a mayor put our schools to the test. New York: Farrar, Straus and Giroux.

This is an excellent book about how three students (who could not read after they graduated from high school) fought the New York Public

School system and won. They proved that it is never too late to learn to read!

Johnson, P., & Keier, K. (2010). *Catching readers before they fall: Supporting readers who struggle, K-4.* **Portland, Me: Stenhouse Publishers.**

The authors have lots of great strategies for helping readers who struggle learn to read easier. They created a bookmark with six steps to remind readers how to decode words and sentences. They put into words what good readers should be thinking and doing.

Rasinski, T. V. (2005). Daily word ladders: Grades 4-6.

The author created fun graphic organizers in the form of ladders to move from an old word to a completely different one.

Rau, D. M. (2007). The Robin in the Tree. New York: Marshall Cavendish Benchmark.

This is a children's book in the rebus (picture-word) format.

Rogers, K., Large, T., Russell, R., & Tomlins, K. (2010). Illustrated elementary math dictionary. London: Usborne.

A math dictionary that has detailed explanations of terms and concepts with pictures and sketches that children and adults will find easy to understand.

Tadlock, D., & Stone, R. (2005). Read right: Coaching your child to excellence in reading. New York: McGraw-Hill.

In the process of learning to read well our brains are constantly searching for prior knowledge to *predict* or *figure out* what will happen next in the passages on a page. The author's intent of this book "... the key to excellent reading ability does not center on identifying words... instead it is centered on the [brain's attempts]...to anticipate or predict the author's intended message." (Tadlock, p.124)

Tantillo, S. (2013). The literacy cookbook: A practical guide to effective reading, writing, speaking, and listening instruction.

Tantillo has a message for teachers and tutors: "If you think about why we read books, magazines, newspapers, etc.—really anything other than a grocery list—it's because we want to learn something. [So]... teach them how to write something that people would actually want to read."(2013, p. 84) I really like this section on page 84, "Punchy Insights Or How To Avoid Writing Like A Robot." And I like how she explains and connects comprehension, reading, writing, speaking and listening together in one book.

Terban, M. (1998). The scholastic dictionary of spelling. New York, NY: Scholastic Reference.

The Scholastic Dictionary of Spelling by Marvin Terban is awesome! It has rules and memory tricks in the introduction for spelling over 15,000 words. "This dictionary breaks words into syllables as they are pronounced. The accented syllable (the one you pronounce a little more strongly) is printed in boldface type." (Terban, 1998, p.4) For example, the word encouragement is displayed as: en – **cour** – age- ment.

Photo Credits

All photographs have been graciously provided by the Pixabay website via https://pixabay.com/. Users can create a free account on the site and easily search for photos by their common names.

"Images and Videos on Pixabay are released under Creative Commons CC0. To the extent possible under law, uploaders of Pixabay have waived their copyright and related or neighboring rights to these Images and Videos. You are free to adapt and use them for commercial purposes without attributing the original author or source. Although not required, a link back to Pixabay is appreciated."

APPLE - https://pixabay.com/en/appetite-apple-calories-catering-1239054/ - CC0 Public Domain - Appetite, Apple, Calories, Catering Meditations /920 Images, *search p. 5*

BEAR - https://pixabay.com/en/grizzly-bear-wildlife-bear-animal-659198/ - CC0 Public Domain - Arthurtopham – *search reference p. 5*

BEARS - https://pixabay.com/en/bear-cub-tree-truck-cute-hanging-79838/ - CC0 Public Domain- tpsdave - *p. 12*

BUS - https://pixabay.com/en/bus-public-transportation-urban-703280/ - CC0 Public Domain - arthurreeder / 3 images - *p. 6*

CAT - https://pixabay.com/en/cat-kitten-young-cats-mackerel-1074981/ CC0 Public Domain - Rihaij - *p. 6*

DOG - https://pixabay.com/en/dogs-heads-makes-posturing-ernst-430192/ - CC0 Public Domain CocoParisienne - *p. 7*

DOG DANCING - https://pixabay.com/en/dog-white-pet-play-dance-733930/ - CC0 Public Domain - AdinaVoicu - *p. 1*

DOG DRIVING - https://pixabay.com/en/cocker-spaniel-dog-car-happy-cool-89247/ - CC0 Public Domain - Capecodprof - *p. 1*

EGGS - https://pixabay.com/en/eggs-egg-easter-white-of-chickens-1289223/ - CC0 Public Domain – ACWG - *p. 2*

FOX - https://pixabay.com/en/fox-grass-wildlife-redfox-nature-335155/ - CC0 Public Domain - IAYDMommi - *p. 4*

GIRAFFES - https://pixabay.com/en/giraffe-out-zoo-brown-yellow-557213/ - CC0 Public Domain - Graver77 - *p. 6*

GIRL - https://pixabay.com/en/little-girl-girl-african-black-563733/ - CC0 Public Domain - Gfergu1

HORSE - https://pixabay.com/en/horse-friendly-equestrian-graceful-824688/ - CC0 Public Domain - succo – *p. 9*

INK - https://pixabay.com/en/abc-leave-filler-letters-ink-442013/ - CC0 Public Domain - 422737 - *p. 2*

JELLY - https://pixabay.com/en/glass-food-purple-grape-breakfast-304543/ - CC0 Public Domain - ClkerVectorImages - *p. 2*

KITTEN - https://pixabay.com/en/cat-maia-animal-grass-pet-cats-832593/ - CC0 Public Domain - benscherjon – *p. 8*

LEOPARD - https://pixabay.com/en/leopard-wildcat-big-cat-safari-518210/ ¬ - CC0 Public Domain – *p. 1*

LIZARD - https://pixabay.com/en/blue-camouflage-forest-green-87560/ - CC0 Public Domain – Byrev - *p. 1*

MONKEY - https://pixabay.com/en/capuchin-monkey-looking-habitat-1187570/ - CC0 Public Domain – Joelfotos – *p. 1*

NEST - https://pixabay.com/en/nest-field-rural-house-landscape-1191609/ - CC0 Public Domain - Ana Sanz – *p. 6*

OWL - https://pixabay.com/en/eagle-owl-owl-bird-bird-of-prey-688025/ - CC0 Public Domain - Barni1 – *p. 6*

PIG - https://pixabay.com/en/piglet-pork-pig-farm-agriculture-520883/ - CC0 Public Domain - Skeeze - *p. 4*

QUEEN – https://pixabay.com/en/queen-elizabeth-i-england-english-62969/ - CC0 Public Domain - WikiImages - *p. 6*

Photo Credits

RAT - https://pixabay.com/en/animal-rat-rodent-408217/ - CC0 Public Domain – Cmon 1980 - *p. 3*

SKUNK - https://pixabay.com/en/skunk-wildlife-portrait-walking-1239764/ - CC0 Public Domain - Skeeze – Skunk tail up - *p. 1*

TIGER – https://pixabay.com/en/tiger-sleepy-zoo-wildcat-relax-695332/ - CC0 Public Domain - Fmlk4u0 - *p. 4*

TURKEY - https://pixabay.com/en/turkey-wheel-california-bird-802234/ - CC0 Public Domain - Smucki - *p. 1*

UMBRELLA - https://pixabay.com/en/screen-umbrella-sky-love-1002156/ - CC0 Public Domain - *p. 1*

VAN - https://pixabay.com/en/mobile-home-vehicle-camper-caravan-157039/ - CC0 Public Domain - Open clipart vectors - *p. 1*

WOLF – https://pixabay.com/en/wolf-canis-lupus-grey-wild-canine-518209/ - CC0 Public Domain - Skeeze - *p. 4*

XYLOPHONE - https://pixabay.com/en/xylophone-musical-instrument-mallets-32128/ - CC0 Public Domain - Clkervectorfreeimages - *p. 1*

YAK - https://pixabay.com/en/animal-hairy-horned-horns-1293769/ - CC0 Public Domain - Jsonbuchner - *p. 1*

ZEBRAS - https://pixabay.com/en/zebras-africa-wildlife-safari-1042615/ - CC0 Public Domain – Seashwill - *p. 1*

ZIP - https://pixabay.com/en/zip-zipper-clothing-fashion-sewing-788929/ - CC0 Public Domain - Jondometita - *search p. 1*

Website Credits

Anne Arundel County Literacy Council. (n.d.). Retrieved June 30, 2016, from http://icanread.org/. Reading Changes Lives.

Every child deserves opportunity. (n.d.). Retrieved June 30, 2016, from https://code.org/ . "Every student in every school should have the opportunity to learn computer science."

Interactive Learning Sites for Education. (n.d.). Retrieved June 30, 2016, from http://interactivesites.weebly.com/

LEARN 3000 WORDS with NEWS IN LEVELS. (n.d.). Retrieved June 30, 2016, from http://www.newsinlevels.com/

Mean mode median. (n.d.). Retrieved July 01, 2016, from https://www.pinterest.com/able4cable/mean-mode-median/

Target the Problem! (n.d.). Retrieved June 30, 2016, from http://www.readingrockets.org/helping/target. Reading Rockets. Launching Young Readers!

Www.ManyThings.org. Interesting Things for ESL Students. (n.d.). Retrieved June 30, 2016, from http://www.manythings.org/.

Acknowledgements

Foremost and above all, I thank my Heavenly Father and Savior Jesus the Christ. Without God's help and love at every step of the way, I would not have written this book. It is also with His help that I made it into and out of graduate school at Florida State University. My motto is "God Rocks Eternally!" Thank You, LORD, for all Your guidance in my life, and especially for the gift of wanting to help others learn to read.

Next, I thank my family: Colin, Ebonni, Jonathan, and Zyonne Beharry for being my anchors, guinea pigs and listening ears through this major book-writing endeavor. Colin put balance in all of the pictures with his design expertise, and Ebonni edited out my wordiness!

I also thank the Anne Arundel County Literacy Council members and tutors for your questions and a working arena in which to test my concepts. I am grateful that I was one of the hundreds of wonderful tutors who work with adult students to bring the joy of reading to others. I am thankful for the students who allowed me to be a part of their learning experiences. I am especially grateful to Mr. M* who gave me new insight into the problems struggling readers may encounter in the public school system.

I thank my pastors, Bishop Antonio Palmer and First Lady Barbara Palmer for the opportunity to get my first book published. You are my heroes!

I also thank Florida State University for the awesome foundation in becoming a School Media Specialist. As a librarian, I get to help readers find the perfect book that pulls them into a story!

All errors found in this manuscript are solely mine and I apologize in advance. Constructive feedback sent to sarahkgardner11@gmail.com is appreciated, and I promise to learn from my mistakes in writing the next book.

-Sarah K. Gardner
June 3, 2016

Author's Bio

Sarah Gardner has a Master's in Library and Information Studies from Florida State University as a School Media Specialist. This grandmother helped her two grandchildren learn to love reading *anything* and visiting libraries. She promotes reading by encouraging others, especially children at church, to read more to improve their grades, academically. Passionate about using suitable materials geared toward students' learning styles to decrease adult illiteracy, Gardner often volunteers as a storyteller for video and audio resources.

She was a volunteer tutor who specialized in finding resources for tutors and students of the Anne Arundel County Literacy Council in Annapolis, Maryland. She recently moved to Augusta, Georgia on a new adventure.

www.ingramcontent.com/pod-product-compliance
Lightning Source LLC
Chambersburg PA
CBHW070543300426
44113CB00011B/1773